OM MOON COLLECTION
by OM WOLF

Wolf Moon

January's Keepsake

Eagle Moon

February's Keepsake

Catching Fish Full Moon

March's Keepsake

Fierce Eagle Moon
you are special to me.
You are the only
full moon in February
that we see.

Eagle Moon, Snow
Moon, Hungry Moon,
Bear Moon in the sky.
Names given by the
Native American Indians,
and the reasons why.

Snow Moon was given as you glow above all the beautiful snow. The beauty of the glow on the snow is quite a spetacular show.

Hungry Moon given by the Native American Indians because of how hard it became to hunt. It was a hard time to deal with the fear of the amount of hunger they may have to confront.

Bear Moon given because the black bears would have cubs in their den. This was a special time for our black bear friend.

Eagle Moon given
because the eagles lay
eggs this time of year.
Beautiful baby eagles are
so precious and dear.

Eagles have a fierce beauty and great strengh to fly high. They are majestic birds that soar through the sky.

My favorite name for
February's only
full moon
that you see
is Eagle Moon
and I like to sing,
"Eagle Moon Watch
Over Me."

Eagle Moon in the sky like a pearl.
Beautifully shining on this world.
You are so wondrous to see.
Beauty for hours, majestic powers.
Eagle Moon please watch over me.
Cuida de mi, watch over me.
Eagle Moon watch over me.

Wondrous eagle Moon representing vision and strength to all. Reminding us to stay on the right path and to stand tall.

Reminding us not to accept the status quo. Reminding us to try our best to see how far we can go.

Fly high and try to reach the sky, each and every day. Be your best in everything you do, in each and every way.

Have the strength to hold your head up high, and the courage to always try to fly.

Be patient with the present you know not what the future holds. Be honest with yourself and remember all your future goals.

Don't be afraid to do what you know is right. Don't ever give up without trying to take flight.

Dedicated
to all the dreamers.
May the moon shine on you
and offer its beauty to
inspire you.

OMFYI.COM

OM Wolf

SCAN ME

SCAN ME

www.ingramcontent.com/pod-product-compliance
Lightning Source LLC
Chambersburg PA
CBHW041603120626
46551CB00002B/297